TOSSED UP
BY THE BEAK OF
A CORMORANT

POEMS OF MARTUWARRA FITZROY RIVER

Beverley-Ann Lupton is the Most Senior Traditional Owner, Tribal Elder and Law Woman for the Gooniyandi Nation. The cover painting is of the artist's Country where she was born seventy-one years ago – the Diamond Gorge.

TOSSED UP
BY THE BEAK OF
A CORMORANT

POEMS OF MARTUWARRA FITZROY RIVER

NANDI CHINNA AND ANNE POELINA

 FREMANTLE PRESS

We are ALL Martuwarra. We are ALL Fitzroy River Watershed.

I share these poems with Martuwarra, Nandi, humanity and Mother Earth.

I dedicate this Martuwarra journey to our young ones. To their world of We Not Me.

We say yes to hearing and feeling 'Voice' to Rivers across the globe.

Martuwarra always was always will be living waters living free.

Professor Anne Poelina, Wagaba Nyikina Warrwa Elder
A Guardian of Martuwarra

I would like to offer thanks and respect to the Bunuba, Nyikina, Gooniyandi, Wangkatjungka, and Walmajarri, traditional owners of the Country in which these poems were researched and written. Many thanks in particular to Professor Anne Poelina, Natalie Davey, Mervyn Street, Carolyn Davey, the Ngurrara Rangers, Joe Brown, Tamela Vestergaard, Natalie McCarthy, and Suzanne Smith, without whom these poems would never exist. Thanks also to the Zoom Zistas: Morgan Yasbincek, Marion May Campbell, Sarah Jones, Suzanne Smith, Libby Angel, and Claire Gaskin for their valuable listening and comments on early versions of some of these poems.

Deepest gratitude and thanks to Martuwarra the magnificent River of Life who has allowed me to get to know her and her many inhabitants and has gifted me the poems in this collection. This project was supported by the Regional Arts Fund WA, Department of Local Government, Sport, and Cultural Industries WA, and the Western Australian Premier's Writing Fellowship 2021.

Nandi Chinna, poet

Contents

Anne Poelina to Nandi Chinna

The River is the first author. The law of the River still stands. The ancestors brought the tree within the limits of the River's country, a bio-indicator of wellbeing. The River is a gift for all humanity to share, a precious and beautiful source of liberation and freedom. You need to form your own relationship with the River as a living system. You need to start talking to the River and then there is waiting time. Wait and it will communicate with you, it will teach you in a dialogic process. Then you can write about the journey of how you engage, how you talk, how you wait, and how you listen.

Blind and Dumb in the Martuwarra – Nandi Chinna

Can I ask you to close your eyes? Better still tie a blindfold over your eyes to block out the light. Then close your mouth and resist the urge to speak. Forget the language you normally resort to. Forget the language you have learned since you were a child. Now that you cannot see, and the language you know has become irrelevant, you may begin to grasp wildly at both of these things, and all that will remain is doubt in its most radical form. You may wonder if you can trust your body, your sensations, your perceptions?

When I moved from the south-west of Western Australia up to Fitzroy Crossing in the remote north-west of the state, my first forays into Bunuba, Gooniyandi, Nyikina, Walmajarri and Wangkatjungka countries felt as bewildering as if I had been gagged and blindfolded. I felt as though I had left Australia, and with it lost all of my familiar languages and strategies as an artist and writer. In reality, the opposite was true. I had arrived in Australia; into some of the ancient, original, and evolving cultures and countries that make up this place now known as Australia. I was born in the colonised south, and despite the courageous efforts of Aboriginal peoples all over the nation, the colonising culture has done its best to cover up the original Aboriginal place of Adelaide. I was born into, and grew up in, an English-style suburb with introduced grasses, plants, and trees, and into English language and culture, with little idea that I was living on the country of the Kaurna people with its own distinct language and culture, and ways of interpreting the place in which it was situated.

In my first few months in Fitzroy Crossing I think I caught a glimmer of what it might take for the kartiya (newcomers/white people) to just step back, to shut up for a minute and listen, which is something that seems hard for us to do. As westerners in the western system, we seem to predicate our identity upon what we can say, not how well we can listen. It's uncomfortable to remain silent. When I walk out through spinifex and termite mounds into the massive plain, I walk towards mountains that don't seem to get any closer. The distances are so vast I could walk all day and still not reach the foot of the ranges. I am ignorant of the names, the interrelationships, the histories and reciprocities. In my own silence, I feel the country shouting back at me. All of my confusion, my failures, my achievements, decisions I have and have not made, the incomprehensible tangle of language, self-judgement, confusion and uncertainty that I carry rises up and explodes in the silence and loneliness of being a stranger in a country I do not know, and that does not know me.

In the vast spinifex plains and ranges of the central Kimberley, the Linnean *Systema Naturae* (The System of Nature), of classification of living things into Kingdom, Phylum, Class, Order, Family, Genus and Species, seems to alienate rather than offer clarity. The Latin and common Anglophone names of those living things are an uncomfortable fit when you try to lay it over the multiplicity of countries and languages you have arrived in.

As Kim Mahood so succinctly articulates, the position of 'kartiya' in the Kimberley is doubtful, even to ourselves.[1]

Walking out in the mornings, the story of the night is carved in red sand: the slash of the snake, the slide of the lizard, and the imprint of its toes laid elegantly either side, plus myriad footprints of beings unknown to me, crisscrossing through the imprints of Toyota tyres and human shoes. This bamboozling riddle of impressions seems to point to my own complicated position as a settler writer and artist living and working in a colonised country. Art making is an ethical act, which requires the artist to rupture and disturb enervated narratives. Walking along this track, I am placing my feet on the path of thousands of generations of Bunuba people's lives, languages and culture. As a descendant of the invading peoples, I feel blind and dumb, and I'm trying to get used to the giddiness of the space left open when I attempt to remain quiet and listen.

My previous creative work has been place-based – poetry generated by walking and trying to remain open to encounters with air, water, weather, terrain, and the voices and habits of different species. As part of this work, I have often been consulting the colonial archive. As I saw it, the question of my responsibility as an artist working in a colonised country relates to finding a mode of representation that is outside of ideas of 'belonging' and its opposite, 'alienation', working in the space that poet and curator John Mateer calls the 'Ontological Predicament of being in Australia'.[2]

Perhaps one aspect of this responsibility is learning how to sit with the layers and complexity of colonisation and bracket them off, to then experience the alienation (feeling dumbstruck) and the separation (from the corpus of the rational). This allows an apprehension of the knowledges and phenomena that have sustained this continent for over fifty thousand years to reverberate.

What all this meant for writing, for my own settler poetics, I didn't know. In place of poetry I made lists of things I see and hear, of questions I have about my own voice. I began to comprehend that new forms and structures, cross-cultural collaborations and conversations are needed to address geo/eco poetics in this colonised Australian context.[3]

After living in Fitzroy Crossing for two years and remaining in a state of uncertainty about whether I should be writing about this place, we attended a concert in the dry riverbed up near the Old Crossing. Elders of all five language groups were invited to speak, and we were also treated to a concert by the legendary Fitzroy Express. We heard from the Elders that the Martuwarra Fitzroy River is under threat from pastoralists wanting to extract water and build dams, which would interrupt the natural flooding and drying habit of this ancient river and damage its unique ecosystems. Fracking exploration is also closing in on the Fitzroy Valley and the trajectory of the sacred Martuwarra Fitzroy River. The ancient spirit of the river, the culture and survival of those living along her is under threat. What struck me most about what all the Elders expressed that night, was that every part of the Martuwarra River is named, and every river place has a story.

Hearing these powerful Elders speak about the spirit and

depth of connection with their River homeplace as we sat, and later danced in the sandy riverbed under a multitude of stars, was a life-changing experience that convinced me even more that there was nothing I could say about this mighty River.

However, the creative impulse is a strong drive, and I felt that I somehow wanted to contribute to the campaign to protect Martuwarra Fitzroy River. In the spirit of respect for the Traditional Owners and cross-cultural collaboration, I phoned Nyikina Elder and Chair of the Martuwarra Council of Elders, Professor Anne Poelina, for some advice about how to proceed. When I explained my dilemma, Anne could not have been more kind and generous. We talked for a while about the river, its cultural and ecological importance, and the threats to its future survival. Anne suggested that I should listen to the river, talk to the river, and then learn to sit in the waiting time, time when this relationship gestates, time for the river and I to get to know each other, and for poetry to arise.

This is what I have done with this poetry collection. I have attempted to avoid the colonial archive, and simply record embodied encounters with the River and its human and more-than-human beings. I hope that by writing this poetry I can share aspects of the personal impact a river like Martuwarra can have on those who are open to listen, both to Traditional Owners and to the River itself. I hope that I have in some way been able to express the extraordinary beauty and magnificence of Martuwarra Fitzroy River and contribute to the ongoing protection of this heritage-listed watercourse which is critically significant globally as one of the world's last wild Rivers.

This poetry collection is a three-way conversation between the Martuwarra River, Anne and myself. As part of this conversation Anne contributes her important poems which carry an urgent message evoking ancestral law and the rights of nature. Punctuating my conversation with Martuwarra, Wagaba Anne Poelina, traditional custodian and river guardian of Martuwarra, shares her poems on Martuwarra First Law, multi-species justice, and the river's right to remain.

References
1. Mahood, K., (2016), *Position Doubtful: Mapping Landscapes and Memories*, Scribe, 2016, p. 44.
2. Mateer. J., (2012), 'Nativism and the Interlocutor', *Cordite Poetry Review*, 1 November 2012, cordite.org.au/essays/nativism-and-the-interlocutor.
3. Minter. P., (2016), 'Introduction to "Decolonisation and Geopoethics"', *Plumwood Mountain; An Australian Journal of ecopoetry and ecopoetics*, Vol. 6, No. 1, plumwoodmountain.com/decolonisation-and-geopoethics.

Martuwarra Time

Martuwarra, the Fitzroy River, tributaries, floodplains, jilas
    and soaks,
mark the sites where *Yoongoorrookoo, Galbardu, Kurrpurrngu,*
    Mangunampi, Paliyarra
and *Kurungal* give life to the Rainbow Serpent's First Law,
    living waters, living free.

The River is watching in the waiting time, waiting to see what
    the humans will do
Lots of talk of Water Planning, Water Allocation, Licences too
Somewhere in there is a hook... uncertainty, we will give some water
to Aboriginal people... not sure what the number is... it's likely
    to displease
They took it from the Territory, 30% was the failed model
    decreed.

What do the people of Martuwarra do?
We know, water markets, water trading, is all about greed.
Greed's got them beat, my Ngoonoo would say,
how could my sister have known what was coming our way
Don't worry about what you can't do!
Get on with what you can!
Her spirit still guides me, and I know she has a Plan.

Living with whiteness, colonialism, divide, conquer,
  manipulate and rule
First the Land, then the slaves, now the water
What's going to be left for Blackfella? was the elder's cry for
  water justice
8th October the United Nations did declare, it's a human right
to live in a clean environment, free from contamination,
  polluted air, misery
Not be poisoned, cheated, defrauded in rules, designed for
  the predatory elite.

Don't ask for a statutory process, procedural fairness,
  distributive justice too
We are in the waiting time, waiting for government and the
  big corporations
who determine the greater good for themselves not
  humankind.
Trade off, water interest not water rights, trade off lives,
those of our kin, the birds, fish, trees, air, and sea breeze.

Canning Basin is shaking from earth tremors over past years,
I still can't believe...
STOP!
This would be the biggest man-made destruction in the world,
Maybe somewhere amongst these grid lines there will be
some happy fat cats, fracking up the River Country
No comparison with the Canada Tar Sands... this will be
  forever wrong

Shale Gas one billion dollar pipeline... which they want to be
  the new song.

Imagine if they invested one billion dollars into our region,
our people, our lifeways, live hoods our economies?
Transitioning coal into renewables, with no new gas
  coming online
No one wants stranded assets to meet the transition energy
  deadline
Songline, singing we want to see, just energy transition for these
  families to be free.

River Country watching and waiting in this modern Dreamtime
Nandi, I know you hear me, you feel me, I feel you too
Write these words down and Dream me to you and we wait for
  the wet to come
Tell the city people about me, tell them all to stand and come.

There are secrets here, I am the largest registered Aboriginal
  cultural heritage site
We have been promised never again, I am fearful ecocide
  and genocide we will become
They don't seem to be listening despite decent human beings
  writing submissions
asking government's meaning of the 2011 song.

Protect Martuwarra Fitzroy River Protect me now and forever,
Martuwarra Fitzroy River... Always Was... Will it Always Be.

They came from the east came with the Songline story in 2011
I belong to the Nation, National Heritage a treasure, diverse
    cultures, and environment
living waters and their guardians all together.

Serpents... swim together waiting for the Waramba and
    the Kajan waters to rise
We wait, we twist up into the sky and down into underground
We hold the Songlines, the stories and the forever memories.

First Law, Warloongarriy Law we all dance, moving and
    rotating the circle
and the men sing the song. Daisy Bates claims Warloongarriy
people danced together to hold the Martuwarra Laws of Song.
When we stand united, we hold the Dreaming time, from past,
    present, and future,
and we sing together a new Martuwarra River Time Song.

At Danggu

If I could remake myself in miniature
I'd climb inside the mountain
tremble with each epoch
each cleft splitting open

I'm one cell > then two >> >>
jelly becoming solid
growing stone from fish racks
my fluids osmose
solidify into white-veined walls
of bone and sinew,

cheeks pressed into Devonian soup
into a submerged world seeping
mitochondrial, oozing milk skin rockface
I crane my neck and look up
into my own beginning

a pale membrane tapers off
into red crenelations
rippled like dinosaur scales
tilting into the water table

my kayak shoots like a red lure
piercing the skim,
vertiginous with falling
into time's deep pools

beneath the trembling hull
primordial species are brining-green,
wimpled eyes emerge/submerge

echoed in its perfect replica
the mountain strokes its twin
daylight plummets and sight turns to wallow
as stars appear like fires burning deep
inside the belly of Martuwarra.

Introducing Martuwarra

An ensemble of birds' voices break
in a morning blue as winter,
blue as crow flight
the river scrawls a circuitous
tannin-stained invitation,

if only I could rest here
inside the river's curled body
spooned and held in sediment,
held in animation,

like spirals of light seeping in through blinds
lapping at my body if not my fuggy mind
sodden with dreams not yet dreamt
and the ones still clinging tenuously
like birds' nests to windblown trees.

Avian song propels me outside
where zebra finches are already
dive-bombing the birdbath
and the air smells of smoke and river.

As we drive across the bridge
I interrupt your sentence
to point and arc my arm
across the expanse of sand and water:
this is Martuwarra, Fitzroy River
the reason for everything.

We all look down into the riverbed,
a haze of smoke vacillates above
two women with babies on their hips
legs planted and taking root
Toyotas lapping at the water's edge
and people motionless like sculptures
tethered to the end of glistening fishing lines.

Martuwarra croons in her rumpled bed
almost like sleep, or a fragment of reverie
almost like a dream yet to be dreamt.

Reciprocal Gifts

Mornings I pedal my bicycle,
mud road noogoora burr scratch
skid huff kite to the river
to work for and receive my gift.

With gloves, knife, black garbage bag
I begin river work:
cut abandoned fishing line from matted nests of driftwood,
gather up anything plastic to break
its noxious journey downriver to Derby
and from there, the Indian Ocean,

sit under the shelter of weeping
paperbark and wait to receive my gift,
a poem tossed up from the beak of a cormorant,
a scatter of sun gems
pitched by handfuls into the stream,
the purling and piping of finches and wrens
in the feathery canopy above me.

Sometimes an unbearable intensity
of life washes over me as I sink
into the sandbank, this river's offerings
almost too overwhelming to receive.

At Dalmanyi (Bell Gorge)

It's not that I want to disappear,
more that I need to drown all other noise,
the annihilating jumble of being and meaning,
cacophony of memory, thought and action,
the opening and closing of screens,
click, apply, OK.

Overarm breaching silk shadows,
out into the vortex of the ice-cold pool
a thunder of white effervescence repeats
like a gif over scarified blocks of stone

weighty plumes of water
hammer my scalp like fists,
punch oxygen from my lungs
delete months from my hard drive,
under I go, with foam in my eyes
held down by the load of the river

all my memories could end right here
in caves of wet darkness
where dogs and birds and old friends
wait to greet me on the other side of sentience.

Churning brown, churning black, I kick up,
shatter this finale into deafening blue sky,
the walls of the gorge glow with afternoon sun
sketched with wraith shadows of teenagers
flinging themselves like bombs from the cliff face.

Impelled by Orpheus

I wander amongst stones
singing to the river
can I charm fossils? minerals?
can I sing water with a guttural wail?

In this song *River* is a sacred word,
I hold it in my mouth like a pebble
roll it, moist and shiny
rattling against my teeth.

Being just one drop in the river's story,
the current is a lyric I can't contain
it butts and crashes against my lips
my lips open and the stones slip
out unstoppable clattering howl

absorbed into the wind
irresistible turbulence
sweeping towards the coast
to mingle with salt
settle into sediment with all
the other notes of emptiness.

The River Doesn't Speak English

Through my perspex mask
I'm trying crocodile view,
a possibility between worlds,

eyes out of focus, the horizon spins
swallowing clouds filled with lightning
sky daubed white with cockatoo wings,
weedy river grass meadows grazed by zebra fish,
four brolgas becoming tree branches,
tree branches morphing into jabiru.

The river speaks in its many dialects.
Still dumb I dive inside it
attempting to unlearn my only language.

Tracking the Two Bodies, Methods for Working With Chaos

There is the memory body,
the one that holds the hoe,
hefts the grain, turns the paddle
through grainy water, strong legs
find foothold on the gorge's rocky walls,
climbing with a billy to make a fire
for tea on the ridge top.

One body remembers rivers, submersion,
deposit and attrition, is touched by both banks
itinerant with the motion of tides,
organ circuitry, source springs,
tributaries in constant relation.

One body is a pencil sketch,
some hours filled in
with intricate shading and crosshatching,
some hours erased,
a grey smudge on paper.

Long unpredictable days
when this body is a crime scene,
a chalk profile of an empty space

inside the white-line shape of a human
with a memory of rivers,
the outline and its doppelgänger,
the completed drawing.

Waramba First Flood

Frogs bark in drainpipes
thunder shocks the heartbeat
the air smells of rain-soaked dust.

In the distance a column of rain
approaches from the west.
From up on the spinifex rock rise
we watch the sky crack open
in blinding scars of light-stitched residue.

Sparks fly from the key
as we unlock the perimeter gate
and run, drenched in seconds,
we make it to the verandah
where our words are snatched
from our mouths by first rain.

Angry Birds

It's early morning and overcast,
the birds flock in to protect their camp
from the human under an akubra hat
perched in the crook of the moringa tree
sawing cuts into soft flesh,
sappy spit, dust splinters,
trying to take one branch to save the tree.

But the zebra finches don't trust this,
nor the yellow-tinted honeyeater,
or the rufous-throated honeyeater.

My old sun-blotched hands are speckled like bark,
my limbs bent into the crook of pithy wood-flesh,
the sky grows bigger with each cut,
patched onto sweaty skin,
dirty t-shirt, hat brim dappled
with freckles of green.

Angry birds descend above me
like a mob with placards – *chee – uck-coo – wee*,
chee – uck-coo – wee, chee – uck-coo – wee.

A hot blue patch opens up in my body
where the fretted branches were,
a too-bright space that we all
must now learn to live with.

On Danggu

The Elders said I should talk to the river,
so I sit on the muddy bank and feel foolish,
tongue-tied, what should I say to this ancient being?

I love you I mutter in blunt English and feel embarrassed,
until I begin to comprehend that I need to be quiet,
to leave my hat, my clothes and shoes
discarded on the edge and slip
into warm water, brown as clay,

sink beneath the surface into myriad
voices speaking in stone,
speaking in lime, in sediment, in fish scales,
in rain coming down from other countries.

That it isn't so much about what I say
but what I can hear and see,
my self contracted to a pinpoint beneath time,
beneath the walls of the sky,
enveloped in something huge,
something so old but continually new.

A sea eagle swoops, talons extended,
grasps the river surface and pulls out silver.

A cormorant drops full-bodied
like fruit from a tree
swallowed by the river's arcane depths.

Inside the reef-caves smell of decades and decay.
A tiny coin-sized turtle turns to meet my gaze,
our eyes held in light suspension

I drift beneath white stone
rippled by antediluvian oceans,
the huge narrative of myself
reduced to one dumbstruck moment
enfolded inside the river's skin.

The River's Work

Martuwarra lies sullen under cloud,
until the sun brushes through
like a watercolourist decorating
each wavelet with sequins of light.

At work again, swelling wide,
she picks up last year's detritus
in a hurry on her way to Derby.

I wade through a rivulet,
shoes off, shoes on,
wobbling across shingles,
Martuwarra is on the move,

she creeps up behind me,
steals my shoes, swirling
like a python around my legs,
Look out!
bending limbs, lemony leaves, marish reverie,
snakes of water with foaming tongues
cut off my retreat.

Suddenly I'm running
the bank is receding
before and behind me
the serpent swallows sand.

Ribs heaving, my pebbly heart
beating in my chest, I'm scrambling
up disintegrating edgings.

Prosodic now, *shoogada shoosh,*
the tug and pull of opposition,
only speaks in relation to resistance,
bubbling ripple swish,
wallaby carcass, bottles, sticks,
residue of other tributaries.

With a tearing sound
she rips huge trees from centuries-
old earth cavities, rewrites her lines
depositing and removing in constant revision
mingling Gooniyandi and Bunuba soil,
blending epochs in her muddy brew.

Sitting on the newly sculpted bank,
heeding the electric buzz of cicadas,
butterflies' silent air painting,
paperbark burrs, *shoosh shoosh shoosh*
pigeons crooning *Bunuba Bunuba Bunuba*
reciting Martuwarra lessons.

Tale of the Bread Bag Tag

From a loaf of fresh bread
on the supermarket shelf
to the sandy riverbed,
the tiny bread bag tag,
white and sharp, lives
for a thousand brittle years.

A traveller on the flood,
sailor on the estuary,
a storm rider cresting and falling
stumbling through tides,
it leaves its land of origin,

stained with river mud it flickers
in penumbral light, pelagic,
never resting, it disguises itself
as an exoskeleton.

Swallowed by a fairy penguin,
it survives her agonising death.
See it there now straddling
a pile of feather and bone
waiting for the next wave.

Australia Day Birds

A flock of budgerigars sprout like leaves
on the grey limbs of a bloodwood corpse,
singing an old song of before Australia.

Green and gold, turquoise flare,
we play statues with the bird tree,
one step – freeze – they halt the song –
we stop – they start singing – we wait,
the song continues.

The horizon is stagnant,
low cloud, diminished sun,
grass quiver, spinifex seed-heads
ruffled and gilded, one more step –

feathered leaves fly from the tree
circle and arc as if in a gust
of green and gold wind.

A kite hawk sits motionless on barbed wire.
When we step too close, it swings open,
dives upwards into its own wheeling cry.

Fairy martins plunge and swoop,
doing fly-bys past our faces
our bodies enveloped in a turbulence
of forked tales and sharp turns.

They stare blackly into our eyes,
our sculptural bodies installed
inside a colony of plumes,
our craned necks giddy with flight.

They circle across the spinifex plain
out to its invisible end
where the day is travelling out of sight,
their wings fusing into fading light.

Adrift

Three brolgas pirouette under the sprinklers
on the nurses-quarters lawn.
The river contracts to shallow pools
and our garden birdbath flutters with crimson feathers.

We watch from behind closed windows
as the sky bleeds rust,
the surface of the land is cast adrift
in a geological movement eastward
a whole nation drifts away.

Until bouldering cloud descends
and a tide breaks above our heads,
drowning out sound
cancelling phone signals
disappearing roads.

The rufous-throated honeyeaters nest
hangs like a wet sock from its mooring
along the moringa tree branch,

the air begins to vibrate
as frogs burrow out of their dry-season nests
with a patter song of trumpet, base, and snare.

At Yirramalay Spring

Two girls having a smoke down at the spring,
us with our camping dust and picnic,
they ask if we intend to swim.

Runnels of limestone and soakage,
360 million years fresh
reborn in air, soft and spongy,
glassy accretion of mossy arteries,
Yes.

We need to welcome you to our country.
We line up, old to young,
baby in our arms,
the girls trickle spring water over our heads,
transparent over our white bodies,
billowing limbs blown like weed,
downstream where black bream nibble our toes.

Water sings louder than thought,
mind hard and dense with logic,
crashing down on shoulder stones
with a roar, drowning out thought,
time and water slap us in the face.

I close my eyes:
time, stone, water
fall across blindness.

My companions say that I look
like a cross between an old
woman and a baby.

With these two faces mirroring
behind my closed eyes
I leap.

On Flying

Seen from above
Earth wears an animal pelt
salt-lake eyes, swamp rivulet
mouth exhales smoky clouds.

Rowdy water stitched this cloth,
with needles of wind, root seams,
deadly set between fire and cloud,
our species impress upon this template,
circulating under our skin, periodic elements,
petri dish, multiply +++ eight billion.

Liquid-scoured salt wounds open
the mountains' stone arteries
dab, daub, circle, eye reprint,
the red fur of Earth's bitten cloak,
skinned, tanned, stripped naked
by ancient ice floes.

Through reed beds, limestone seepage,
rise tender shapes, a vascular system
of half-moons and circles,
fanning out across distance, carving
coral eyes, fossil trees, ferny reef beds
across interiority; this Earth animal
shifts and sighs, lurches and exhales
beneath the wake of flight.

Storm Eggs

Teenage girls sit
cross-legged on the riverbank
and all talk is of the river rising
up under the bridge chocolate-coloured,
broiling, drowning and resurrecting treetops,
spreading out, turning roads into seething tributaries.

In the scud of each footstep
clouds of blue butterflies
brume up from newly sprouted grasses.

From the verandah an alarm insists
through diamond-shaped spaces in the cyclone fence,
an industrial-strength choir of frogs,
erupts from ephemeral waters.

The dusty golf course transforms overnight
into a clicking chirruping lake.
Ghost-white tree trunks unfurl their reflections,
perfectly articulated branches and leaves
ripple on the evening's mirrored surface
where a few days ago I rambled,
puffs of dust arising in the aftermath of every step.

All this life arrives instantly
through bolts of lightning
exploding inside anvil-shaped clouds.
In the morning, new eggs lace the birdbath,
shiny black dots that soon grow rudders,
navigate in circles around the watery
orb of their containment.

Rainbow Bee-eaters

Riding home at dusk
the horizon haemorrhages into grasslands
welding the edge of earth to sky.

Clouds buffet and bend in fluid light,
the black-stilted water tank
feet astride, holds hard against evening.

Upon powerlines plucked by wind
a flock of rainbow bee-eaters
land and alight, harmonic,

their collaboration plays along my skin
opening pores, quivering follicles,
unsealing my ribs like the pages of a sacred score.

In the morning when I cycle out again,
the rainbow opens its wings,
a spectrum of primary notes
erupting from roadside trees.

Martuwarra Kingfisher Camp

Streaks of opal cannon
across the river,
call and response
five-tree morse code
in a smoker's gravelly rattle.

It's good for our eyes
to squint into the distance,
sitting by a cup-of-tea fire
on the riverbank
the earth turns fast enough
for us to observe Orion
slipping beneath the tree-line.

Celestial bodies ignite in the river
as we sit and wait for the moon.
Is it under there somewhere?
deep in weed and mire,
soggy with flood?

While we wait, the water
lights up with red crocodile eyes
their submerged bodies
hovering beneath the river's skin–
red-steady-go buttons
illuminate the riverbanks like an emergency runway,
for a landing entangled in stars.

Interrogating Moon

I never thought to put it down to the moon,
the restless re-runs of well-rehearsed scenes,
a projector rolling backwards
through the cinemascope of my life.

But there you are, it had to be,
because there I was
lying awake under the thin veil of a mozzie dome
on the banks of a restless river
with the spotlight of the moon
glaring into my face like an interrogator.

Who are you really?
a huge epic crammed into the skin
and muscle of a failing body?
Or a chain of unrelated scenes
strung together vicariously?
Do you have a use-by date?
Or a best-before?

Tree shadows loom like grasping arms,
spiders with diamonds flashing in their eyes,
scuttle away from their own silhouettes
while down in the dry-season river
a flotilla of crocodiles hunt.

My pulse races through my body
like a startled horse. Lunar rays
burn through closed eyelids
and question me again,

Who is it that resides in your body?
Are you the same you that you were as a child?
Will you live long?
Will you ever be loved?

All night that flaming satellite
tosses me through the stony rapids of myself,
until it drops into the river with a slow sigh.

I crawl out of my swag and stoke
the ashes of last night's fire,
stare into the river that swallowed the moon
now lit with strobing kingfisher flight.

Melaleuca Afternoon

Lying fallow in a paperbark grove,
the sky framed by parchment limbs,
on one side infinity, underside of kite hawk,
blue-winged lace butterflies,
the sandy riverbank subsides
into the contours of my animal.

Trying to guess which bird
makes which song
their madrigals are medication
as good as, better than sleeping
more restful than dreaming.

We pad down the sandbank,
fishtail into the sepia-toned river
fresh-skinned and velvety,
shallowing west towards salt.

I fill my hat with water and douse myself,
my hat fits better now.
Campfire smoke spools from the riverbank
through this one culminant human encounter
in the lifespan of a river,
a red dragonfly dazzles the air.

Danggu Evening

Cliffs plummet into their echoes
the river yawns with sky-black trembling
a space fabric rippling with candescent
coals of burned-out fires.

Rocks highly prospective for zinc, lead deposits,
petroleum extends into the subsurface biography
of a U-shaped reef built by limestone secreting organisms.
(how I turn from night walking to googling
to supplement my evening stars Danggu knowledge)

The vinegary odour of bat piss
pale splashes of guano
dusky-winged shadows glide
through a purpling sky
while we watch the Devonian reef disappear
into shadows of temporal elasticity.

In the blackness between stars
rocks are forming and dissolving,
a water bird *whoop whoop whoops*
into the crevices and below,
a saurian wallow.

Crickets ring like tinnitus
awaiting the moon's rise
for the cosmos to become a river
for the river to open its briny maw
and devour the laving of an ancient sea.

Singing Yoongoorrookoo

I am Yoongoorrookoo, the singing Rainbow Serpent,
travelling high up in the sky and down through the rivers,
the air and the sea, the river and the soil.

I feel a great sadness now carried by many people
They cry out and ask, what is happening in our Nation,
    in our Country, in our home?
I see below me floods and fires crisscrossing the land,
    big storms and harsh heat
Our knowledge of Country ignored by government
    and bureaucracy
Wake up, I say to you, and hear my belly crawl
Wake up maybe one last time and listen to
    Bruce Pascoe's call
There's wisdom here, heavily rooted intrinsically between
Aboriginal nations, their land, living waters, sea, and sky
Aboriginal voices being muted in their protection of our rivers,
crying out, we need to be recognised.

Defrauded, dis-eased into staying quiet,
Now through their mourning, awakening others to their calling,
recognised, reconciled, and healing, a united transformation
in order to fully nurture the Australian Nation

This Australia, taken by theft from a lineage of
   ancestral custodians
It's time to pause and take a deeper breath.
Rivers must have a right to life and their contribution
to all other life must be respected.

Some are fearful the humans lead their own extinction
I have hope in human beings, for living water lives
   within them too
It's their life they must save if they are to continue living on
   Mother Earth
Mother Earth covered in living waters cradled beneath the sky
I keep on singing as I believe a coalition of hope is coming
The Martuwarra Fitzroy River Council is calling
   a circle of Elders,
wise people from across the nation to come to our
   River Country
Share the stories of development, protection, and
   new economies,
culture, conservation, science, tourism, renewable energy
This can be a future.
Let the policy reflect these northern-development
   Indigenous dreams
and plans for growth, investing in sustainable and fair trade
   through Indigenous hands
Traditional owners are standing up, supporting economic
   growth and prosperity

Heaven knows how hard it has been, enslaved, poisoned,
    imprisoned and dispossessed,
stripped of their lands since George Grey's 1837 expedition first
mapped these western frontier estates.
Surely now don't come to them with an unsustainable
    Fitzroy River management plan.
Stand together in good faith, free informed consent
Stand with the Martuwarra Fitzroy River Council for a fair go
A circle of Elders could hear these stories and frame new ways
    to build the forever industries
Industries grounded in climate science, human rights
    and environmental justice
Cooperation, not conflict. Unity, not divide and conquer
Collaboration, not manipulation, cultural synthesis, not
cultural invasion.

Done hand in hand with fellow Australians, reaching out
    to global networks
to achieve the Paris targets and transition from
    fossil fuels to renewables
Valuing the sunk cost investment of this globally
    unique Fitzroy River
a riverine system not found anywhere else on the planet.
Stop the invasion, the continuing colonisation
Let's recognise the original West Australians
Their right to freedom and justice upon their tribal estates,
Recognise them for their collective wisdom, science,
    farming, engineering,

medicine, and healing, diverse trade innovation and ceremonies.
Indigenous nations believe they have a fiduciary duty
    as custodians and guardians
Legislative river protection acts across the whole Country
This must be done before it's too late
Earth jurisprudence, First Law
Law of the land.

This is the cry from the Aboriginal nations of this
    wide brown land
This has been the message championed through the rivers of
    the Murray Darling Basin
Rivers have the right to life, they must flow free
This must become a Nation's songline if the Australian
    bloodlines are to hold
the past, present, and future strong
I sing this to you, singing the River Law song for
    people and Country.

In the long hours of the night

how many of us are lying awake
mourning for rivers that no longer flow,
for the gaps in the playlist,
so many voices deleted
from the soundtrack of dawn?

How many of us when we finally fall
into a restless kind of sleep,
dream of birds we once knew to herald our mornings,
now reduced to the utter loneliness
of a single unaccompanied song,
or a meticulous drawing in an out-of-print ornithological journal.

To be the last of your kind, and then the last.

The extant wild river pulses in my temples,
wakeful as her current flashes through me
I'll hold on through every bend,
each riffle and waterfall, submerged sandbank, and reef cave
as she spreads out across her floodplain
and pummels against the caterpillar legs of the bridge.

There are people on the banks
from Mornington to Derby
whose lives hold the river's memory
and the brolga fishing in the pebbly shallows,
where will she go when the last wild river is gone?

I wish there was a remedy
for the loneliness of the last wild river,
perhaps only to wade into the flow
to hold the river's life in our hands
let it pour through, let its worry
become our worry, its survival
become our work.

The Unbearable Weight of the Road I

Riding along Danggu through the ochre
streak between daylight and stars,
trees shudder with feathered storm-harbingers
racketing up lightning, white Prado music

booms into the dip of a dry creek bed,
tail-lights disappear, high beam, *thump,*
an agile wallaby winded on the road jolt,
front leg collapsing, inky eyes glazed,
her mate shuffling in the verge-side grasses.

Bicycle wheels spin on the verge,
headlights blind down on a human crouched
fingers grasp sticky fur
slide a hand into her dank pouch
no joey, hold
her steady as she vomits up
the unbearable weight of the road.

The Unbearable Weight of the Road II

Then it's Grand Final weekend,
Noonkanbah Blues VS Muludja Lions,
fans convoy towards Fitzroy
through a blur of spinifex and tarmac,
past many-breasted termite mounds
like Venuses of Willendorf
arms outstretched between Derby and Fitzroy Crossing

three Toyotas, two caravans, jumbled on the roadside,
a woman holds a red shirt like a kite
shadow stretched to block out the sun,
a woman with her head in hands
crouched like a cardboard cut-out
pasted onto the blue floating air
the golden grass stems,

red dirt roadside where a girl has flown,
in a split second her bones turn to air
her West Coast Eagles shirt whirling
plumes of gold and blue
out of the shattered car window.

A woman from Melbourne clasps the elbow
of the quaking driver stride to stride,
a first-aid kit is produced,
someone radios for help
as trucks thunder past
gusting our hair and clothes

our shock bent sideways, my arms
ache high, fingers as sutures return a face to its skull,
a busload of evangelists in dusty clothes
stop to lay their hands upon our shoulders.

Red shirt kite,
woman kneeling in the grass,
pushing breath into a torn
West Coast Eagles shirt.

Kite hawks alight from wallaby deconstruction work,
diminish into distance, dark missiles
vanishing through a gap in the Erskine Range.

Time builds mountains as sirens
and lights fail to appear
along the endless scarred macadam.

Where the River Once Met the Sea

As soon as I sink into the water
I begin to drift on the flotsam of myself,
the fizzing tide navigates me
ballooning like sea grass
towards the shore.

I think about the Jabirr Jabirr people
whose country I am immersing myself in,
the many stories I can't see
beneath sandy eddies scouring
waterlogged stones.

Submerged in the salt life,
old pop songs surface in my mind,
I feel my complicated arrangements
wash off me like accumulated grime.

Crowded with my own lineage
my blood jangles with the things I can't shake off.
The ocean picks up my body like driftwood,
spins me sideways into gentian-violet distance,
humming a tune as land disappears and I go
with the tide, sinking and rising
inside each beckoning swell.

On Leaving Fitzroy Crossing

One minute I'm sitting on the edge of Martuwarra
staring into stygian depths where stars
are flickering on like the lights of a metropolis,
campfires flare along the riverbank
illuminating figures held like statuary
on the land-end of barramundi.

Next minute I'm in the back of a taxi
in a tributary of headlights
stop-starting along Tonkin Highway
with petrol fumes choking the window gap,
and red-tailed cockatoos screaming
over piles of woodchip mulch.

Then I'm in Coles with Mum
pushing our trolleys, we cram
through the fruit and veg, plums on special,
minds addled with choice.

In the pet-food aisle
endlessly bright and plasticky,
crocodiles, emus, camels, kangaroos,
cows and horses are sealed into cans and packets.

One moment I'm paddling a red canoe
through Martuwarra floodwaters
amongst tree canopies
where the river employs a new geography,
frantic insects cling to holey leaves,
coiled snakes dangle from ngiyali trees,
drowned fence lines barbed to scratch.

Along a sunken track onto Plum Plain,
now a tabular sheen, a drowned field
of windblown grasses cooking to kelp
under the shadeless lamp of mid-morning,

we skim past a crocodile swept up in the wash,
fish broken out of the riverbed,
losing navigation in a submerged woodland,
then I'm overboard swallowing Martuwarra
in minerally gulps.

I lose Mum in the confectionary section.
Emerging with a jumbo block of chocolate,
we *dit dit bop, dit dit bop* through the checkout,
our trolleys swing like dodgem cars on the sloped paving,

back in the glittering torrent of cars
rushing towards and away
carrying cargoes of clatter and rustle,
the smell of diesel lodged in my mouth
like a boulder in a creek,
stepping on the throat of my song.

Olga the Brolga

No one knows the answer
to the question of why her beak
crosses itself like pincers, like a mouth
that has said too much,
that's just how she arrived,
with another grey chick
and survived.

At first her mate fed her,
stabbing fish and bugs
into her complicated mouth,
down her flower-stem neck.

Now it's we who,
legs astride her back,
hold the bug mix in one hand,
open the beak with the other,
and like snooker balls descending
shove down meat down in lumps.

She flies down to the river
sometimes disappears for days,
until we see her again,
dancing at her own reflection
in the car window,
spinning at the bottom of the verandah steps,
performing her ballet for a feed.

Listening
(with permission of Mr Joe Brown)

Out on Djugerari the clamour of town
fades into an immense distance,
the febrile blue of limitless sky,
red mountains stitched together
with blazing needles of spinifex grass.

Sam is yarning to Uncle Joe,
You know uncle, when I'm on my own country I can see,
I can see where the animals are and have been,
I know where I am.
When I'm on your country,
I'm blind, I can't speak
because I don't know where I am.

Well, Joe says, *when we visit*
someone else's country we wait.
If we are asked to speak, we do.
If not, we stay silent.

Within our dome of firelight
the wood speaks its burning,
the planets overhead articulate their turning,
sprays of stars strewn
as if spat from the mouth of an enormous deity.

All around us night settles,
through the spinifex plains,
yet the grasses seem to hold a memory
of the day's glaring luminescence,
lapping like a bristling gilded ocean,
against our tiny island of flame.

Driving from Djugereri to Yakanarra

sunset obliterates the wheel ruts,
and I'm driving blind, a troopy full of women
singing along to Dolly Parton and her *coat of many colours*
these *girls just wanna have fun*,
the Rocky Ridge Band serenades Yakanarra
and I wonder if that song will get us there.

Underground, swarms of termites
dismantle and rebuild the desert.
Terracotta light bounces off their chimney-stack nests,
ignites stalks of spinifex that sway
like a field of lava lamps.

We stop to scout for firewood
as the road fades into night
and I'm hoping the Toyota
knows its own way home.

The stars are skittering above
when we pull into the community
nestled under Old Woman's Hill.
The men have lit a fire and cooked
the roo hunted as they travelled.

I make another of my faux pas
and sit with the men around the fire.
Everyone falls silent until I pick up my chair
and move to the women's circle.

In the line-up for stew, M nudges me in the ribs,
I knew my playlist would get us here.
I wander down along starlit tracks
to the kartiya camp and crawl
into my mozzie dome with
corrugations rattling in my limbs,
the Rocky Ridge Band on repeat in my mind,
where the desert glows at night, oh Yakanarra.

Sacred Waterhole, Yakanarra

This morning the fire rangers
are being welcomed to this Country.
We head out in a convoy of Toyotas
only to find the station people
have been busy with a bulldozer
clearing a track through the swamp fringe.

The Elders are distraught.
What can we do?
We hunt around, find a black poly pipe
protruding from the mud,
the sacred spring leaking from its ruined mouth.

We line up, an odd bunch,
pink-skinned TAFE lecturers wearing inadequate caps,
fire-smudged countrymen and women,
we step forward one by one
bow our heads like confessors at an altar
as the old woman pours Living Water over our heads.

It tastes metallic and muddy,
I shake my wet hair
and the welcome sprays out in shiny droplets
catching the glint of the windscreen,
a flock of brolgas, necks outstretched,
scattering silver arrows into a livid sky.

The Drowned World

On the way upriver we hardly speak,
partly because of the noise of the engine
partly the rising immensity inundating our thoughts.

Up to Danggu, engine whining
through banks of grey cloud
helmswomen spot dislodged trees and other flotsam
coursing down towards Fitzroy.

Baz is at the helm,
coat on, coat off
he peers over the rim of his rain-blinded glasses
navigating the toy boat
bobbing in a churning brown bathtub

or are we the bathtub spinning
on the river's girth grown fat
spilling out of its clothes,
tree limbs splayed
across an underwater sky?

The engine groans upstream,
and all our maps are sunk,
our signposts submerged,
our mouths full of rain.

Water cascades down rock faces
as our tiny vessel time-travels into Danggu,
ten metres up the cliffs into black rock
what is the metaphor for flood?
Baz and Barb in sodden matching polo shirts?

Drenched in seconds we are porous
beneath spluttering waterfalls
decanting from flooded caves
where we once paddled our kayaks,
all drowned now, all retreated
to the new limen in the treetops.

Talking About Rivers

Yesterday we talked about rivers,
how the river would miss its people
if they were gone, how the people
would grieve and long for the river.
When you asked the old people about Waitangi
they said *Martuwarra is not a person*
'E an ancestral spirit.

You told me how you needed
to take some water from Martuwarra
and pour it into La Meuse in France,
for these two ancient rivers to meet,
talk to each other, *Hey we need help*
  if we're gunna survive we gotta work together.

The sound of water was deafening.
We had to shout over the voice of the river
speaking in syllables of flood and retreat
in five different languages,
five different names all meaning the same thing,
telling of what happened before
hydrology and geology were invented.

You said this is not just the story
of what's on the ground,
of what you can see,
but what's underneath
running like arteries, like subplots,
the bones of the present moment
in which we and our talking
are just one iteration of breath.

You said the water belongs to the river
to the beings that live along her,
to the people of the river.

We finished our tea and walked out into the street,
the river still fluent inside us, Martuwarra
welling up in our mouths.

Nesting

Along dry season's wide edges
we dig out a small nest
set twigs for a fire.

This is where we come
the same dusty bank
to watch egrets hunt in the gravelly current,
wallabies alert sipping while the sun
paints the river bloodshot and inflamed.

All is birds' wings fanning the air,
river tongues drubbing through shallow rapids
no human language seems adequate
so we lie, our bodies moulded into the river's mattress
lapsed into galaxies of sand and flame
purling into echoless space,

where winds are soft against our skin
then howling with the fury of risk,
dying only to be reborn
in the kindled fire,
the warm breath of the river.

After three months away

in the cold and rainy south,
returning to Martuwarra in the morning by bicycle
old tracks have been redrafted by flood,
fresh drifts of bulldust, new sandbanks,

but the alabaster shudder of the pelican
still wades in snakes of light on a particular bend,
the jabiru still impales the shallows with its sharp beak.

I grab a stone and rub it into my armpit,
cast my respects to the Elders,
my salutation rains into the sun's flare,
throwing speech bubbles of river
into palpitant air.

And what of this river?
It welcomes me back with caution and gravel,
and a flock of kite hawks circling my every move.

Remembering *Papillon*,
I yell into their orbit
I'm not dead yet!

Kite shadows dip and glide,
their glittering kohl eyes fixed upon me
a small paisley-shirted figure,
stomping and sinking in sand.

Washed-up killer bones remind me
that I too will one day be reduced to fragments
of mandible and jaw, calcium and crystal,
as I wade through the water that gives and takes away.

Fishing

I always wondered where the stars go
when the bolshie sun barges up
out of the treetops and elbows them out of the way.

Today I discovered them
trapped inside the river's shallows,
still sparking, still flaming
in their watery confinement,

until along comes the jabiru
stalking on her knobbly red stilts
she steps through watchfully
up to her knees in idols

shaking her enormous black beak
she runs, wings outstretched,
dances a few steps and gobbles
the slippery universe
one glossy planet at a time.

Meditation Music

Skirling through its renewed trajectory
Brooking Creek performs a melodic hum,
double-barred finches provide the high notes,
whistling kites, a kind of gyratory melody.

While I squat and expel my body's water
my phone rings and it's a friend from Sydney,
the creek's opus bounces up to a satellite,
through an infinity of space to the east,
where she asks if I'm playing a meditation CD.

A balmy wind breezes from the main river
and it's hard to believe during the wet season
we drove a boat up here, our heads ducking
and brushing the footbridge now eight metres in air.

That this was all swallowed beneath the flood
and we could hardly hear our own shouting,
above the wild brown dog of torrent bolting,
all action and sweat.

Now I'm sitting mutely, waiting
while ants crawl into my clothes
bee-eaters and finches decide I'm a mannequin
and swoop down to graze their beaks in the flow.

Corellas, kite hawks, white-faced heron, sacred ibis,
names for feathers and flight, drumming skywards
trailing tendrils of bravura from their dripping talons,
the percussive sound of their wing beats
land an ephemeral pulse in lotus pose body.

How foolish we are

to deny change,
to think that our parents will always be
there in our childhood homes
in rooms full of books
that we tell ourselves
we will eventually read.

We comprehend how the river
changes its course every year,
a new sandbank humps into the bend,
it may not be the same
great egret haunting the flinty shoals?

When flood rewrites the river's arc
our camp is buried under acres of water,
the track tapering off into muddy suffusion.

Yet we walk on through our lives
ignoring the dried bones
washed up along the riverbank.

Each day my mind runs through its plans,
feeling satisfied if the words have come out right
while always there lurks the encrusted lime and weeds
that I am and will become.

From Martuwarra's verandah

a searing opal of light
so many songs careening in river trees
a busy world of morning survival
the working day begins, to find a feed,
sing pollen and insect sap,
snatch flies from midair fanning,
suck nectar from creamy flower stamens
and disappear back into leaves
when the shadow of the whistling kite
paints over the sun.

Four brolgas sail down Brooking Creek
and land like ceremonial dancers
in the stony shallows of Martuwarra,
dip their long lotus-stem necks down/up

in a choreographed performance
they step downriver, breakfasting as they go
towering through the crowds of sacred ibis like royalty
they dip and wave, fish and drink
until the river meanders out of view.

12 Days Until Christmas

and look what the flood has revealed:
a decades-old ute rusting in the sandbank,
massive trees thrown across old tracks,
newborn plateaus, dunes and shoals,

fresh steepness, footprints in mud
the creek scours a half-moon
of silt into the river channel
last year's snags raft downstream
past a huddle of ibis returning.

I lie down in the creek, accommodating,
warm like amniotic fluid the water parts
at my skull and rejoins across my feet,

muddy residue sifts into my clothes
and before long I'm being dive-bombed by
fairy martins: wrens
hurtle down the creek line
drop into the bends
wings open, holding their bodies
to a drowsy air current.

My eyes, cut out of sky fabric
have fallen into my face, opening
momentarily I comprehend where I am.

Martuwarra Fitzroy River Flood 2023

a translucent baby
gecko on the kitchen benchtop,
wallabies huddle on verandah
boards *slap slap* a cow knee-deep
in the back of a waterlogged ute

the road is gone, we live
on islands Rivered from the world
wade out from our houses,
storm clouds surpassing our stride

there are no hierarchies
brown whorls have eaten that
laved path an untrackable scent
we don't know where to place

our feet mud enters our marrow
for the first time the years, the centuries
the oldest heart in the fossil record
Gogo fish's earliest awkward
galumph out of Devonian swamps

mould grows up the walls
slosh through the supermarket
aisles rattle cages empty shelves
float out   drift out

terror looks the same in any animal's eyes
going under lungs filled with sludge
we watch from the bridge
the river's thunder knocks out pylons

furred ones with human animal eyes
a column of bats kilometres long
tears apart the bleached sky
dragging broiling rainclouds
upriver behind them.

Islanded from each other
by the loss of our starry skies
our animals and their iridescent country
pouring now out into King Sound

the lights go out   darkness laps
over the edges of our apprehension.

Reading back to Martuwarra

River words have swept through my keyboard
churned the rugged mill of the thesaurus
the strain of syntax, punctuation, *tap tap*
mudlark, cockatoo, ibis.

River words have sunk deep
dried to mud crusted over,
been buried by kartiya worry and shame
sediment finally settling then un-
settling again inside the next flood.

Martuwarra has been performed
to audiences in the south
Nyikina Nooloo on Zoom
and now the woman
of the River says *it's time*
to read your poems to Martuwarra,
let her have the final say.

Cold-time puffer jacket
billy and tea things, poems
to the Old Crossing where I light a fire
squint over the lip of my mug
into the sun's spill and warp,

four brolgas hunt-dance upstream,
I throw in a pebble and call out my name

wade out ankle-deep, my wad of paper
stained with mud, imprinted
with the tracks I've been following,
reciting lizard prints, croc slides,
three-toed chirography
a white body the page/my voice
disperses into Martuwarra's flow.

What are the Humans Doing?

*Yoongoorrookoo, Galbardu, Kurrpurrngu, Mangunampi,
  Paliyarra and Kurungal*
our sacred serpent beings are twisting up in the sky
Down into the ground asking the question
What are the humans doing?

Watch for the Kajan waters from the Waramba she told me
Ngabarl calling Ngabarl storying
How could my ngoonoo my sister, Lucy Marshall remember
  all the things to say
Don't drink that dirty one dirty Waramba flood gonna come
Learnt from the past to dream the future now
Listen to the River Country, it can be cruel it can be kind.

Waramba Crying Martuwarra Sighing
Right now, in 2023, it's turned upside down, making us dizzy
  you and me
Fitzroy River Disaster the news flash tells the world to see
Fitzroy River Crossing bridge collapsing, emergency services
COME QUICKLY
Visit by our Prime Minister and Premier who came to see
Flood Relief... Flood Recovery
Immediate need is to settle misery.

Our Balginjirr still in the waters, it's a Disaster Zone
    my brother tells me.
Turning and twisting and wondering why
Looking for meaning up in the sky
What are the humans doing?
Don't blame Martuwarra Fitzroy River
I never made this flood
Bureau of Meteorology can tell you
It's human induced
We going to get more intense rain
Temperature and sea level already rising
This is no climate change hoax.

Climate change is real, people
Climate chaos and climate wars are the new normal
Why is it so hard to see with our ears?
Listen with our eyes!
Our rules of Wunan told us from long ago
Relationships, respect, reciprocity, responsibility, ethics
    of caring, love and peace
Wunan from an artist from Sunrise to Sundown Country
Send Jarmandi 'Big Red Kangaroo' to sing to us
Let us hold this First Law Song

The old ones are passing this knowledge to young ones
Hold love in your heart, your liyan, your moral compass
    to guide you through life

Don't worry there's plenty out there to destroy you
    if you don't stand for peace
How can we have this when the people who hold the money
    and power don't see
What we dream and feel free?

River Country is crying asking the human to be kind
Look at all your own stories of how you can do this right now
Nature Reserve Systems to protect and promote
Watersheds
We've already done this
It's a Commonwealth policy until 2030
Bioregional Frameworks it's part of the reset
My friend Greg Campbell agrees **TOTAL RESET**
Makes the point this is what we need!

Indigenous and non-Indigenous young people cried out
    to our Nation
We can't live in a Nation which refuse us a duty of care
Minister for the Environment don't be unfair
Our right to inherit inter-generational equity
Our future inheritance to enjoy this Nation is still our plea.

Kooya, Mother told me if we move the people
The bureaucrats and in turn the politicians will understand
Maybe the big greedy Corporations could develop
    an ethics of care too
We must wake up the people is the cry of the snake

If the people are united have informed consent
Together we will understand the cumulative impact test
Climate chaos and climate wars are real
We need to learn to be climate resilient
Adapt a Bioregional Plan
Adopt the Watershed known as Dampierland

Wunan Law in modernity a cooperative bottom-up story
Local government could be the new normal with investment
    to cope
A chance for a Bioregional approach
A focus on the Martuwarra Watershed as we have done
    from the beginning of time
Now maybe at last we can all stand united, cooperating,
    being informed
for our greater good, not somebody else's plan

No more Waramba Crying
No more Martuwarra Sighing
People Place and Nature and Living Systems not dying
We can all be part of the trying
We all want the same things and for our young people
Reach their potential and privilege their voices to Dream free
I write this for my Kamirda grandson and for
    David Suzuki's grandson too
We must not be crying wondering what we are leaving them
We should be like our Martuwarra singing.

Martuwarra sing and swim and flow you will be here in the
future
We promised *Yoongoorookoo, Galbardu, Kurrpurrngu,*
   Mangunampi,
Paliyarra and *Kurungal* to give it a go
Then these sacred serpent beings can say
We sing we dance up in the sky and underground
When we stand united with One Mind and One Voice
Ngabarl said '*shoulder to shoulder,*
Sorry 'bout that we still got our culture,
We still gotta role to play'.

See what our human family can do!

Martuwarra Quite Contrary

Martuwarra Martuwarra
Right to Flow
Right to Live
Right to Gift
Giver of Life
Martuwarra Martuwarra
Quite contrary
Ask the people how will Martuwarra flow and live

When it comes to decolonisation and contested spaces
If we don't know how
We just keep on doing what we know
A gift is not a gift until it is given
A life well lived contains memory past, present into the
future
Martuwarra Martuwarra flow free
Martuwarra help us to see the We in Me

How? is the question,
A wise man said.
Sometimes we ask this question too soon
The Answer to How is Yes!

Dreaming Yes
Dreaming Me to We
Dreaming One Country
Country Dreaming with One Voice

Martuwarra
Gift to humanity and Mother Earth
The Gift
A Total Reset
Dialogic Action
Cooperation
Unity
Organisation

We share Mother Earth
We send the Dream out
We continue
Sing... dance and ceremony upon her girth
We share love... wisdom... Peace
Love our Pluriverse

Nandi to Anne (via text)

Nandi: I'm standing in the river reading poems to Martuwarra.

Anne: Thank you. I am on my community at Balginjirr. I'll listen out for them coming down.

Glossary

Balginjirr – Pandanus Park Community is a Nyikina Aboriginal community, located sixty kilometres south of Derby in the Kimberley region of Western Australia, within the Shire of Derby–West Kimberley. It is on the banks of the Fitzroy River.

Bunuba – people of Bunuba country, which stretches over 6,500 square kilometres in heart of Western Australia's West Kimberley region, along the Martuwarra Fitzroy River. bunuba.com/bunuba-country

Dalmanyi (Bell Gorge) – is located in the Wunaamin Miliwundi Ranges Conservation Park in the Kimberley region of Western Australia on the country of the Wilinggin and Bunuba people.

Danggu – Bunuba name for Geike Gorge.

Djugerari – is an Aboriginal Community located on Walmajarri Country, 110 kilometres south-east of Fitzroy Crossing.

Dreaming – an active time to manifest transformation to visualise the future in the now. To send a dream out and find others to walk with you while you dream together what can be. What can be created, transformed with dialogue, actions, and hope.

Dreamtime – the fusion of time, bringing together lived experiences and memory from past, present and future into this moment in time, right now.

Fitzroy Valley – the Fitzroy Valley is 2,500 kilometres north of Perth and 400 kilometres east of Broome, in the remote Kimberley region of Western Australia. Fitzroy Crossing town is the main shopping and administrative centre. The Valley is home to approximately 4,500 people, eighty per cent of whom are Aboriginal, belonging to five language groups – Bunuba, Walmajarri, Wangkatjungka, Nyikina and Gooniyandi. Kimberley Kriol is a common language. There are forty-five distinct communities in the Fitzroy Valley, ranging from larger communities (300 people), to small Aboriginal cattle station communities with as few as ten to twenty people depending on the season. See marulustrategy.com.au/pages/the-fitzroy-valley.

Galbardu, Kurungal, Kurrpurrngu, Mangunampi, Paliyarra, Yoongoorrookoo – different Aboriginal names for the Sacred Ancestral Serpent being known, since colonisation and white settlement, as Fitzroy River.

Gogo Fish – the Gogo Fish, *Mcnamaraspis kaprios*, is an extinct placoderm of the Late Devonian period 380 million years ago. It inhabited the ancient reef systems of north-western Australia and grew up to fifty centimetres in length. Intact fossil specimens of the Gogo Fish were discovered in the Gogo formation in the Fitzroy Valley, which was an ancient inland sea during the Late Devonian period. Internal organs have been found in well-preserved specimens, including the oldest heart in the fossil record. See paleozoo.com.au/Gogo-Fish.php.

Gooniyandi – Gooniyandi country is located in the central Kimberley region of Western Australia and includes the Margaret River, Martuwarra Fitzroy River and its tributaries. Gooniyandi country covers more than 11,000 square kilometres of land and water and includes the Indigenous-owned pastoral stations of Bohemia Downs, Mt Pierre and Louisa Downs and portions of the non-Indigenous Christmas Creek, Gogo, Fossil Downs, Larrawa and Margaret River pastoral stations. Gooniyandi country is roughly bounded in the north by the Margaret River, Christmas Creek and the Great Sandy Desert in the south, and the Fitzroy River to the west. See gooniyandi.org.au/about-us/about.

Jabiru – black-necked stork, *Ephippiorhynchus asiaticus*.

Jarmandi – Big Red Kangaroo who carries First Law of the Land not of Man, from Sunrise to Sundown Country. The top of the Fitzroy River Watershed is sometimes called the 'Ranges or the Hill Country' through the mountains of Mt Wynne, Mt Anderson, Mt Clarkson and Mt Jowlenga to the Dampier Peninsular.

Jila – living water, waterhole.

Kajan – the turbulent 'dirty water'; the first flush of the river following the first wet season rain.

Kamirda – grandmother and grandchild reciprocal relationship.

Kartiya – non-Aboriginal person.

Kaurna – Kaurna Meyunna are the Aboriginal people of the Adelaide region. Kaurna Meyunna Yerta the Kaurna peoples' traditional tribal land, or Country, extends from Cape Jervis to the south of Adelaide to Crystal Brook to the north, and from the Mount Lofty Ranges to the coast of Gulf St Vincent. See charlessturt.sa.gov.au/community/arts,-culture-and-history/kaurna-culture/kaurna-country.

Killer – colloquial term for bullock or cow.

Kooya – Nyikina word for 'Mother'.

Kurungal – see **Galbardu**.

Kurrpurrngu – see **Galbardu**.

Liyan – wellbeing of spirit, body, culture and country. Yawuru language.

Mangunampi – see **Galbardu**.

Martuwarra – Martuwarra or Mardoowarra is the name that Nyikina people give the Fitzroy River. The Bunuba name for the river is Bandaralngarri.

Moringa – *Moringa oleifera* is a fast-growing, drought-resistant tree of the family Moringaceae, native to the Indian subcontinent.

Muludja Lions – Muludja Community football team. Muludja is a small Aboriginal community, located twenty kilometres east of Fitzroy Crossing. It was established as part of Fossil Downs Station and relocated to its present location in the early 1980s. The current site is an excision from Gogo station, close to the Margaret River and boundary with Fossil Downs station. With a current estimated population of approximately 155, most residents speak Gooniyandi, but other languages spoken include Kriol, Walmajarri, Bunuba, Kitja and English.

Ngarbal – traditional name of Anne Poelina's sister, Lucy Marshall AM. See also **Ngarbal** in References.

Ngiyali tree – (*Bauhinia cunninghamii*), Bunuba language.

Ngurrara Rangers – the Yanunijarra Ngurrara Rangers are based at the community of Djugerari in the southern Kimberley region. They are an Indigenous Ranger group who look after the Ngurrara native title area, including part of the Canning Stock Route, the Warlu Jilajaa Jumu Indigenous

Protected Area (IPA), in accordance with cultural protocols and guided by Ngurrara Traditional Owners. yanunijarra.com/rangers

Ngoonoo – sister, Nyinkina language.

Noogoora burr – a native plant of the south of North America, Mexico and the Caribbean. It was first noticed in Australia on Noogoora Station, Queensland in the 1870s, where it was probably introduced as a contaminant of cotton seeds. It has since spread over much of Queensland and New South Wales. Other infestations occur in Victoria, South Australia, the Northern Territory and certain sections of the Kimberley in WA. See: agric.wa.gov.au/declared-plants/noogoora-burr-what-you-should-know

Noonkanbah Blues – football team of Yungngora Community, situated on Nyikina country at the southern boundary of Noonkanbah station on the banks of the Fitzroy River. Traditional languages spoken are Walmajarri and Nyikina, and the more recent language of Kimberley Kriol.

Nyikina Nooloo – Nyikina dance on Zoom.

Paliyarra – see **Galbardu**.

Rainbow Serpent – see **Galbardu**.

Walmajarri – the Walmajarri people traditionally lived in the Great Sandy Desert to the south of the Kimberley but since colonisation have gradually moved out of their country to cattle stations and towns in the north of Western Australia. The Walmajarri are part of the Yi-Martuwarra Ngurrara Native title claim and since 2007 have incrementally won native title over an area of approximately 20,000 square kilometres. The Ngurrara native title holding group is comprised of people from the Walmajarri, Wangkatjungka, Mangala and Juwaliny language groups. See klc.org.au/native-title-map.

Wangkatjungka – Wangkatjungka is a community situated 100 kilometres south-east of Fitzroy Crossing. The community is located on an excision of Christmas Creek Station and is a settlement of predominately Wangkatjungka-speaking people. There are about 180 permanent residents of Wangkatjungka, and the people are Walmajarri and/or Gooniyandi, proud people with strong links to their river and desert culture. See org.au/our-communities/wangkatjungka.

Waramba – first wet-season flood, Walmajarri language.

Warloongarriy Law and Wunan Law – First Law governs the responsible management of the Martuwarra watershed through Warloongarriy, the Law of the River, and the Wunan, the Law of Regional Governance. The Warloongarriy ceremony re-enacts the Woonyoomboo story, when the ancestor being Woonyoomboo speared the serpent, Yoongoorrookoo, who created Martuwarra in the Bookarrarra, the beginning of time. Warloongarriy Law recognises all people living within this unique living hydrological watershed as one society, calling us Warloongarriy people, bonded in a moral contract of goodwill and good intent to protect the Martuwarra Watershed through a bioregional governance approach. The Wunan Law is a Kimberley-wide network of reciprocal, place-based sharing and ceremonial exchange, based on cultural leadership, which reinforces kinship ties and extends people's social world through an ongoing circulation of goods and ceremonies. Since Bookarrarra, Warloongarriy and the Wunan Law have provided a framework for understanding the central role of water in all things, and its relationships to everyone and everything around us. A polycentric bottom-up governance model of custodianship and an ethics of care and love to promote and protect Martuwarra/Mardoowarra's right to live and flow. See also **First Law** in **References**.

Yakanarra – Yakanarra is a small Walmajarri Aboriginal community approximately sixty kilometres south-west of Fitzroy Crossing in the Kimberley region of Western Australia.

Yimardoowarra Marnin – a woman who belongs to the Martuwarra/ Mardoowarra.

Yoongoorrookoo – see **Galbardu**.

Notes and References for Poems

'Martuwarra Time'

30% was the failed model decreed: The Strategic Aboriginal Water Reserve (SAWR) describes a reserved percentage of water from a Water Allocation Plan area (such as Martuwarra) that is available to local Aboriginal people with 'eligible rights' for use or trade. The SAWR is capped at 30%.

UN declaration: On 8 October 2021, the UN Human Rights Council recognised access to a clean, healthy and sustainable environment as a universal right.

Canning Basin shaking and fat cat fracking: The Fitzroy catchment sits on the Canning Basin, which is the largest shale gas reserve in Australia. Only two percent of WA's land is legally allowed to be used for fracking. In October 2021, the WA state government offered American oil and gas company Bennett Resources an exemption, which would allow fracking in the National Heritage–listed catchment.

Canada Tar Sands: the Athabasca oil sands contain the largest deposit of crude oil on the planet, and they sit on First Nations land near Fort McKay in Alberta, Canada. The natural environment in this region has been destroyed and is so heavily polluted that it's labelled 'ecocide'. See 'Ecocide must be listed alongside genocide as an international crime', Alexandre Antonelli and Pella Thiel, *The Guardian*, 23 June 2021, theguardian.com/environment/commentisfree /2021/jun/22/ecocide-must-be-listed-alongside-genocide-as-an-international-aoe.

Shale gas is considered an 'unconventional' gas, which means it is trapped underground by relatively impermeable rock. Hydraulic fracturing (fracking) includes drilling holes into the earth and fracturing rock with a high-pressure fluid mixture to release the trapped gas.

decent human beings writing submissions refers to the tens of thousands of submissions made on the WA Government's Fitzroy River Water Discussion Paper calling for the entire length of the Fitzroy River to be protected and for no surface water to be taken from the river or its tributaries.

The 2011 song: In 2011 Martuwarra / Fitzroy River was listed as a National Heritage site under the *Environment Protection and Biodiversity Conservation Act 1999 (Cth)*. See Commonwealth Government. 2011. 'Inclusion of a Place in the National Heritage List: The West Kimberley'. Canberra, ACT.

Daisy Bates (1863–1951): welfare worker and self-taught anthropologist who extensively documented the life and customs of First Nations people in Western Australia and South Australia.

'Tracking the Two Bodies, Methods for Working With Chaos'

This poem was inspired by writings in *Being Bodies: Buddhist Women on the Paradox of Embodiment*, Lenore Friedman and Susan Moon, eds, Part 4, 'Three Methods for Working with Chaos' by Pema Chodron, and Part 5 'Tracking the Two Bodies' by Toni Packer and Lenore Friedman (Shambhala, 1997).

'Singing Yoongoorrookoo'

Bruce Pascoe's call: '"We need to act and we need to act now." Mr Pascoe said it was time we took responsibility for the planet the way Aboriginal people had done for more than 120,000 years. "If we can we'll have prospering health, we'll have a prospering economy and we'll have prospering societies."' Alex Crow, 'Commission for the Human Future calls for action on global catastrophic risks', *Canberra Times*, 19 September 2020, canberratimes.com.au/story/6847251/prominent-australians-call-current-crises-warning-of-whats-to-come.

Martuwarra Fitzroy River Council was established by Traditional Owners as a collective governance model to maintain the spiritual, cultural and environmental health of the catchment, advocating a collaborative approach for an inclusive water governance model and catchment management plan.

See ANU Research Publications, 'Martuwarra Fitzroy River Council: an Indigenous cultural approach to collaborative water governance', A. Poelina et al., openresearch-repository.anu.edu.au/handle/1885/287975.

George Grey: British army lieutenant who carried out an exploration of the Kimberley.

Paris targets: The Paris Agreement is a legally binding international treaty on climate change that was adopted by 196 parties at the UN Climate Change Conference (COP21) in Paris on 12 December 2015. See unfccc.int/process-and-meetings/the-paris-agreement.

The Murray Darling Basin is a system of interconnected rivers and lakes in the south-east of Australia. More than 2.3 million people live in the Basin, including people from over fifty different First Nations groups. Anne Poelina was the inaugural appointee to the MDB's independent Advisory Committee on Social, Economic and Environmental Sciences.

'On Leaving Fitzroy Crossing'

stepping on the throat of my song adapted from a poem by Vladimir Mayakovsky, 'At the Top of My Voice', 1930. marxists.org/subject/art/literature/mayakovsky/1930/at-top-my-voice.htm.

'Driving from Djugereri to Yakanarra'

'Coat of Many Colours' is a song written and recorded by American country music singer Dolly Parton. It was released on 27 September 1971, by RCA Victor.

'Girls Just Wanna Have Fun' is a song written and recorded by Robert Hazard and made famous by Cyndy Lauper, who released her version on 6 September 1983 under the label Portrait.

'Yakanarra' by the Rocky Ridge Band, 2017, Triple J Unearthed.

'After three months away'

Papillon is a novel written by Henri Charrière, first published in France on 30 April 1969.

'Martuwarra Fitzroy River Flood 2023'

On 30 December 2022, remnants of Tropical Cyclone Ellie brought days of torrential rain and wind to northern Western Australia, which caused Martuwarra to reach record-high levels, inundating floodplains, destroying infrastructure and isolating riverside communities. On 4 January 2023, the river's water levels near the town of Fitzroy Crossing peaked at a record high 15.81 metres. See earthobservatory.nasa.gov/images/150814/flooding-along-australias-fitzroy-river. This poem was first published by Red Room Poetry, 2023.

'What are the Humans Doing?'

Fitzroy River Disaster: See 'Martuwarra Fitzroy River Flood 2023' above.

First Law song: 'First Law is the collective body of Laws of the First Peoples of the land mass currently known as Australia. It is the body of laws which have governed relations between and within First Nations and between the human and non-human since the beginning of time. It is undisputed under First Law that the River Country of the Martuwarra has an inherent right to life. At the same time, adherence to First Law is fundamental for realizing the Martuwarra's continued right to life. This is the foundation for recognizing the River's right to life and correspondingly the need to recognize the rights of Traditional Owners to co-manage the River as guardians so that they can fulfil their responsibilities to present and future generations.' See aph.gov.au/DocumentStore.ashx?id=b2f57e40-f0a8-4d40-93b3-5bb4 daff22d3&subId=691040. See also **Warloongarriy Law and Wunan Law** in Glossary.

Commonwealth policy to 2030: *Australia's Strategy for the National Reserve System 2009–2030* is an Australian Government document from the Department of Climate Change, Energy, the Environment and Water aimed at protecting the nation's biodiversity. See dcceew.gov.au/environment/land/nrs/publications/strategy-national-reserve-system.

Bioregional frameworks were established by the Australian Government's Department of Climate Change, Energy, the Environment and Water dividing Australian land mass is divided into 89 bioregions and 419 subregions. See dcceew.gov.au/environment/land/nrs/science/ibra/australias-bioregion-framework.

Dampierland is an interim Australian bioregion in the West Kimberley. The Fitzroy catchment is located in the Dampierland bioregion. See dcceew.gov.ausites/default/files/env/resources/a8015c25-4aa2-4833-ad9c-e98d09e2ab52/files/bioregion-dampierland.pdf.

David Suzuki is a Canadian academic and environmental activist. His grandson, Tamo Campos, was arrested for protesting Kinder Morgan's gas pipeline expansion on Burnaby Mountain, British Columbia.

Ngarbal, 'shoulder to shoulder […] we still gotta role to play' was the title of the inaugural oration of the Chair of Indigenous Studies when the life of Lucy Ngarbal Marshall AM was celebrated for her contribution to research with respect for her leadership, wisdom and life of practice. 'A dignified wise woman, with the power to commit to memory generations of cultural knowledge and practice, Ngarbal dreamt that we would all act and work together to share our spirit, liyan.' See researchonline.nd.edu.au/nulungu_workshops_presentations/02/schedule/1/.

Sources and Acknowledgements

Publications and films can be viewed at Anne Poelina's website **annepoelina.com**. View stories, action, and the interactive map on the Martuwarra Fitzroy River Council website **martuwarra.org**.

To write her poems, Nandi drew on the following:

Ballard, James G. (1962), *The Drowned World*, Berkley/Medallion, New York.

Brown, Joe (2023), interview, Fitzroy Crossing, Western Australia.

Davey, Natalie (2021), interview, Fitzroy Crossing, WA.

Martuwarra Fitzroy River (2019–2023), in dialogue and encounter.

Oscar, Mona, G. Brooking, D. Chungai et al. (2019), *Yarrangi Thangani Lundu, Mayi Yani-U: Bunuba Trees and Bush Foods*, Environs Kimberley Incorporated, WA.

Playford, Phillip E. in D. Hopley (2009), *Devonian Reef Complexes of the Canning Basin, Western Australia*, dmp.wa.gov.au/Geological-Survey /Devonian-Reef-Complexes-1538.aspx. Full text: researchgate.net/ publication/262697269_DEVONIAN_REEF_COMPLEXES_OF_THE_ CANNING_BASIN_WESTERN_AUSTRALIA_Geological_Survey_of_ Western_Australia_Bulletin_145_Devonian_ammonoid_biostratigraphy_ of_the_Canning_Basin.

Poelina, Anne (2021–2022), in conversation, Fitzroy Crossing, WA.

Street, Mervyn (2021), interview at Mangkaja Arts, Fitzroy Crossing, WA.

A version of 'Blind and Dumb in the Martuwarra' was published 10 July 2019, by the Sydney Environment Institute.

The poem 'On Danggu' first appeared in *Plumwood Mountain Journal*, vol. 10, no. 1.

'Martuwarra Fitzroy River Flood 2023' was first published by Red Room Poetry, 2023.

About the Authors

Nandi Chinna works as a research consultant, creativity facilitator and poet based on Bunuba and Whadjuk Noongar countries. She received the 2021 Western Australian Premier's Writing Fellowship for her project *Two Rivers: First Nations Voices on Rivers and Wetlands*. This project utilises a decolonising methodology which primacies the voices of First Nations people. Nandi is the author of *Swamp: Walking the Wetlands of the Swan Coastal Plain* and *The Future Keepers*, which was shortlisted for the Prime Minister's Literary Award and the Victorian Premier's Award for Poetry.

Professor Anne Poelina, Citizen Nyikina Warrwa First Nations, PhD, PhD, MEd, MPH&TM, MA, Chair and Senior Research Fellow, Indigenous Knowledges Nulungu Institute of Research, University of Notre Dame. Adjunct Professor, College of Indigenous Education Futures, Arts & Society, Charles Darwin University, Darwin, Peter Cullen Fellow for Water Leadership. Anne is the inaugural First Nations appointment to the Murray–Darling Basin Authority Advisory Committee on Social, Economic and Environmental Sciences (2022). She is a member and Visiting Research Fellow of the Institute for Water Futures, Australian National University; and is a Member of the Commonwealth Department of Climate Change, Energy, the Environment and Water as part of the Committee on Aboriginal and Torres Strait Islander Water Interests. In 2023, she was nominated as Ambassador for the Western Australian State Natural Rangelands Management, and in 2019, was a founding member of the WA government's Aboriginal Water and Environment Advisory Group. In 2018, she was the inaugural Chair of the Martuwarra Fitzroy River Council. Anne has been recognised for many of her achievements and contributions, including receiving a Laureate (2017) from the Women's World Summit Foundation, Geneva; the Women Taking Climate Action Award (co-winner 2023); and the Kailisa Budevi Earth and Environment Award, International Women's Day (2022) in recognition of her global standing.

First published 2024 by
FREMANTLE PRESS

Fremantle Press Inc. trading as Fremantle Press
PO Box 158, North Fremantle, Western Australia, 6159
fremantlepress.com.au

Cover artwork by Beverley-Ann Lupton
Designed by Karmen Lee, Karma Design, hellokarma.com
Printed and bound by IPG

A catalogue record for this book is available from the National Library of Australia

ISBN 9781760992804 (paperback)
ISBN 9781760992811 (ebook)

Fremantle Press is supported by the State Government through the Department of Local Government, Sport and Cultural Industries.

Fremantle Press respectfully acknowledges the Whadjuk people of the Noongar nation as the Traditional Owners and Custodians of the land where we work in Walyalup.